**KEEP THE MAN YOU'VE GOT!**

D0003217

*Treat Your*

# MAN

*Like A*

# V.I.P.

*By Xcavier T.*

**TOPLESS TACTICS YOU WERE NEVER TAUGHT**

# Author's Note

The names and other identifying characteristics of
the persons included in this book have been changed.

Centurion House, LLC

2751 Verbena St.,
New Orleans, Louisiana 70122-6039

Cover photo and back cover image by Gus Bennett
Author photo by Carlton Mickel
Designed by The Printers' Wholesale Group
Manufactured in the United States of America.

ISBN 0-9759050-0-7

# TABLE OF CONTENTS

# Acknowledgements

Special gratitude to Yvette Foy, whose faith and friendship helped carry me to this expected end. I would also like to thank my classmates for their honest opinions that continue to calibrate my ego and make me a better writer—especially Sean Patterson.

This book is dedicated to my parents and children, who demonstrate daily that love covers a multitude of sins. Thank you for loving me unconditionally through my evolutionary process, for I shall never be found worthy.

# Preface

*Treat Your Man Like a V.I.P.* grew out of the numerous hours I spent entertaining in V.I.P. rooms of an upscale gentleman's club on Bourbon Street in New Orleans. Having been a wife once myself, I was surprised to find the majority of my topless bar clients were married businessmen who sincerely loved their spouses.

What motivates men to seek entertainment in gentleman's clubs? Follow as I disclose my personal experiences. I'll never again meet as assorted a group of men as I met while working as a stripper. Bourbon Street caters mainly to tourists, which helps to provide the topless bars with a continuous flow of business travelers from various regions of the world: men from America, men from China, men from Australia, men from Germany, men from India and men from Spain to name a few. There are always dysfunctional characters that visit gentleman's clubs, such as the client who pays four hundred dollars to be kicked in the testicles; but these men are not the norm. Most of my clients were married professionals who were more than willing to flash a wallet-size photograph of the wife, kids and the dog. Though the pictures were always perfect, the relationships often were not.

Each encounter with my gentlemen clients was a unique experience, yet the stories that they shared about the state of their relationships sounded almost the same. As a woman who had failed at love in the past, I was intent on soaking up every complaint until I had gathered enough information to develop a plan that would help to guarantee the success of any marriage. If one couple can be saved or one family better united because of my plan, then that fact in itself shall be my reward.

*Most of my clients were married professionals who were more than willing to flash a wallet-size photograph of the wife, kids and the dog.*

### *Character Dossiers*

Individual state laws govern the topless bar industry in the United States, but local politics will help determine the eclectic offering of adult establishments in your area. There are bars with showers, bars with lap dancing, bars with both topless and bottomless entertainment, bars with private floors known as V.I.P. floors, bars with private rooms known as V.I.P. or champagne rooms, and these are only some of the options. V.I.P. areas are set apart from the main floor and can be accessed either by paying additional fees to both the dancer and the bar or by being an established patron. The different varieties of topless bars are made more fascinating by the array of customers. From the dancer's point of view, there are many categories of male clientele who visit topless bars, but I have narrowed it down to three: The Regular, the Sugar Daddy, and the General Public. Where does your husband fit in? I'll let you decide...or perhaps you already know.

*The Sugar Daddy can be a dancer's "bread and butter," or more realistically her "rent and car payment."*

### The Regular

There are patrons who are routine visitors to upscale gentleman's clubs. These men are as knowledgeable about the inner workings of the topless industry as most of us girls, if not more so. The Regular doesn't necessarily have a fondness for a particular dancer; but he does have an affinity for topless bars, and he visits them whenever and wherever he travels. It is highly unlikely that the Regular would be hustled by anyone; in my experience, it's the Regular doing the hustling. This is a man committed to getting the most value out of his dollar. There is a mutual respect between the experienced patron and the experienced dancer. Just as the most astute day trader can accurately analyze the fluctuation of his tech stocks, the seasoned Regular can spot a willing dancer who's two martinis away from lowering her price in the V.I.P. room.

While it may seem strange to consider such a well-informed customer an asset to the dancers, understand that this breed of male sets the tone and atmosphere inside the club. Depending on the depth of their shyness, a roomful of novice customers can easily translate into loss of revenue for both the dancer and the establishment; whether due to nervousness or guilt, novices can be intimidated by their enjoyment of unfamiliar naked women in the company of unfamiliar fully clad men. The Regular, on the other hand, has overcome this obstacle and he inspires other men to conquer it as well. Never underestimate the contagious nature of positive energy. One table full of festive Regulars can be as thrilling as a Mardi Gras parade and generate as much excitement as the game winning touchdown.

*Why the General Public enters these establishments is not nearly as important as their reaction to the girls once they are inside.*

## The "Sugar Daddy"

The Sugar Daddy is a Regular of a different sort. The Sugar Daddy is that patron who is consistently generous with the same dancer on each visit. They frequent the club as often as the Regulars, but when these Sugar Daddies arrive, every dancer knows who they are and which particular girl they're in the club to see. If a Sugar Daddy is a big spender, his dancer will halt any other patron's negotiations and cater to him exclusively. The Sugar Daddy is well aware of his role and happily performs it to the extent his wallet will allow.

The Sugar Daddy can be a dancer's "bread and butter," or more realistically her "rent and car payment." Dancers share an unspoken code of honor never to hustle another girl's Sugar Daddy without her permission, and any infraction of this rule is probable cause for bodily injury. I have witnessed quite a few spats in the dressing room because someone refused to respect the stripper code of ethics as it pertains to the Sugar Daddy.

While some dancers see the Sugar Daddy as money in the bank other dancers think of them as health hazards. As in any other relationship, there is a level of emotional commitment involved in cultivating a Sugar Daddy customer; and depending on how frequently he visits a dancer, how much time he spends with her, how much money he spends on her, and how he views her psychologically, unintentional and often unwanted attachments may occur. Dealing with a Sugar Daddy can be like walking a tight rope: it's an emotional balancing act where the slightest bobble can send everyone crashing.

An experienced dancer can convince her Sugar Daddy that the money he pays for her time is only a technicality; if it were not for the bill collectors breathing down her throat, she would have no interest in it whatsoever. This type of effective role-play can unleash a succession of unfortunate events. Both the Sugar Daddy and the dancer have now ensnared themselves within an elaborate tale that each party is willing to perpetuate with the misconception that everyone's emotions will remain in check. Once the Sugar Daddy allows himself to believe the fantasy that the money is anything other than payment for services rendered, he can no longer maintain objectivity and self-control. No longer is the Sugar Daddy in a business relationship if he has persuaded himself he is in love.

I have seen both sides of the Sugar Daddy debate. I've known the relief of seeing my Sugar Daddy stroll into the club on a not-so-exciting night and the thrill of having one evening with him bankroll my bills for the month. But, I have also suffered the debilitating fear of dealing with the ones who wrongly determined they were entitled to my emotional loyalty.

## The General Public

A majority of the remaining male population would fall into the category of the General Public. The General Public consists of men who only visit gentleman's clubs on special occasions, such as bachelor parties, going away parties, conventions, or special outings with clients. Why the General Public enters these establishments is not nearly as important as their reaction to the girls once they are inside. If inspired by the right personality type, some members of the General Public lapse into autopilot and find themselves quickly transformed into a zombie like character that they barely recognize.

On numerous occasions, I can recall meeting clients who reluctantly came into the club at the urging of their colleagues, and later found themselves spending $400.00 to be alone in a private V.I.P. room with a girl they'd just met. These men don't know why they deviated from their original plan to have a drink and maybe one table dance. While the reasons remain unclear to the customer, the girl in the V.I.P. room with the $400.00 knows!

No one is born a Regular or a Sugar Daddy. These patterns emerge over time. If your husband is a part of the General Public, and has yet to have a V.I.P. experience in a gentleman's club, the application of the topless tactics in this book will help ensure that he remains that way. If you treat your man like a V.I.P. nobody else will have to do it for you.

**KEEP THE MAN YOU'VE GOT!**

# Treat Your

# MAN

## Like A

# V.I.P.

### By Xxavier T.

**TOPLESS TACTICS YOU
WERE NEVER TAUGHT**

*Chapter 1*
# GUERRILLA WARFARE
*The fight to preserve your marriage*

Despite what you may have read in books and women's magazines, seen on talk shows and internet sites, or heard from psychologists and relationship gurus, it is much easier to get a man than to keep one. If you are married now, or have been in the past, then you have probably already come to the same conclusion. All around, women are waging campaigns more extensive than the Battle of Normandy trying to obtain a mate: they take in all the literature, participate in seminars, attend seances, go on game shows, and fall for any number of internet gimmicks all with hopes of nabbing a man. No suggestion is too far fetched as long as it produces the desired result.

> *Women are trained to focus on a wedding instead of the marriage itself.*

## THE TURNING TIDES

Unfortunately, once victory day arrives, the energy level that went into capturing him is not maintained to keep him.

Women are trained to focus on a wedding instead of the marriage itself. Most are unprepared for what happens after the "I do." To their surprise, women struggle to maintain even a fraction of the friendship they once enjoyed with their mates. They won the battle to conquer the territory they now call "husband," but are clueless about the Guerrilla warfare that awaits them: increased responsibility of an expanding family, greater involvement with an aging parent, unexpected financial woes, or the callous advances of other women are some of the skirmishes they will face. Whatever practice or technique you employed to snag your man is of no consequence now. You may have won the battle, but major uprisings rage on. If you allow yourself to forget this important piece of information, you may find your spouse in the enemy's camp.

TREAT YOUR MAN
— LIKE A VIP —

# ORDINANCE #1

## TO KEEP YOUR MAN
## YOU NEED A RETENTION PLAN.

★ Keep your enthusiasm about your relationship consistent.

★ Your mate should remain your first priority even if your family expands.

★ Your relationship is a perpetual work in progress.

## Chapter 2
# KNOCKOUT DROPS
*Wielding a seductive scent*

It was my first night as an exotic entertainer, and I wanted everything to be perfect. I had all the anticipation of a virgin bride planning her honeymoon, though none of the chastity. I labored over every detail imaginable. What color dress would I wear? Should the dress be long or short? What type of thong panties would I wear? Should the thong be hi-cut or low-cut? What type of jewelry would I wear? Should I opt for a choker or a collar? My hands and feet were also an issue. Should I don fingernail polish, toenail polish or both? And shoes, I couldn't forget those. Opened or closed toe stilettos? My last decision was perfume; the scent had to be just right. I was the product, but packaging was everything.

I finally decided on a long, red, evening gown. It had a halter-shaped top with an empire waist that gradually flared toward the bottom, neither too tight nor too flowing. I wore a red garter and red velvet T-back panties. Red worked well with my skin tone, complementing my complexion under the stage lights. Besides, all the vixens in classic cinema wore red. I chose a skinny rhinestone collar over a choker, because it hinted at the potential to misbehave without looking overtly sleazy. The shoes were open-toe stilettos and the fragrance was Chanel No. 5—classic, elegant. I sprayed it everywhere: my shoes, my feet, my thong, my garter, as well as my hair, my breasts, my butt, and my inner-thigh area. This might seem like overkill, but I knew I would be competing against the smells of cigar and cigarette smoke, alcohol, natural body odors and cheap cologne sprays.

Finally, I made my debut. Everything was going well. I was sitting at a table with several other performers and a group of men. One of the clients at the table said, "Your perfume smells familiar." This is a great sign, I thought to myself, validation that I had made a quality choice of fragrance. A few moments later the man proclaimed, "I know why your perfume smells familiar. My grandmother used to wear it!"

*When properly wielded, a scent can be a great tactic of Guerrilla warfare. It is an opportunity to stimulate your mate without making a move or whispering a sound.*

All the time I had thought I smelled sexy, and here he was thinking of me as an old lady. I learned a lot about perception that night, and it was the last time I wore perfume older than me.

## PERCEPTION IS IMPORTANT

Fortunately you have only one man to please. It's much simpler to get the fragrance right. What smell reminds your mate of you? Is it baby drool? Bacon grease? Cleaning products? Doggie snacks? These are not the aromas you want your mate to associate with his adoring wife.

FROM THE TRENCHES ★ ★ ★ ★

*I had a client for whom I was very careful to wear the same fragrance every time we met. It ignited such joyous memories that whenever he thought he smelled my perfume on a stranger, he would stop them to ask the name of their fragrance.*

If your man were five hundred miles away and caught a hint of your perfume on another woman would he be compelled to call you? Or at least think about you? If one whiff of your scent does not stop your mate in his tracks wherever he may be, then you are neglecting the bonding instrument of smell. When properly wielded, a scent can be a great tactic of Guerrilla warfare. It is an opportunity to stimulate your mate without making a move or whispering a sound.

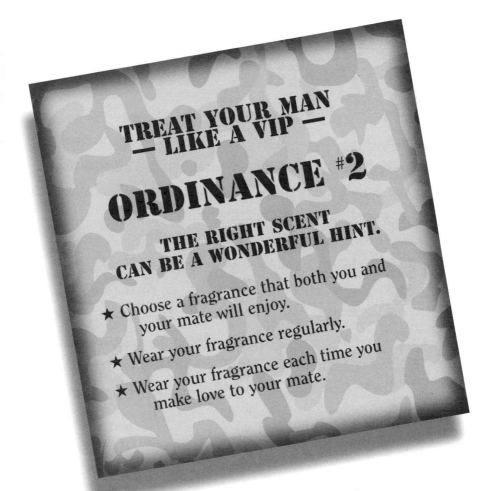

TREAT YOUR MAN
— LIKE A VIP —

# ORDINANCE #2

### THE RIGHT SCENT
### CAN BE A WONDERFUL HINT.

★ Choose a fragrance that both you and
your mate will enjoy.

★ Wear your fragrance regularly.

★ Wear your fragrance each time you
make love to your mate.

# Chapter 3
# MP PATROL
*His place of refuge within the home*

The bedroom should be the most sacred quarter of your home, and the very thought of it should fill your mate with unreserved anticipation. Imagine your bedroom as the General's quarters. It is his final place of refuge, one he shares with his most trusted comrade—you. The General does not come here to hear complaining about the republic, grumbling about the aesthetics of the territory, or griping about the misdeeds of the little military brats. The bedroom is a haven from the cares of the world, and you alone are the guardian of this sanctuary.

> *The bedroom is a haven from the cares of the world, and you alone are the guardian of this sanctuary.*

If you have not yet established any bedroom guidelines, now is the time to commence. Consider your bedroom a No Fly Zone. Repeat after me: "I will not fly off the handle in the bedroom area." Discuss family matters outside of the bedroom. Keep your discussions within some other space you have appointed. If you are conversing about a matter and have not found resolution, set an agreed-upon time and place to continue the dialogue. Keep your word and drop the conversation until the designated time. This tactic gives both of you an opportunity to rethink your stances on the matter, and preserves what should otherwise be a pleasurable and peaceful night.

## BURY OLD HABITS

Initially, it will be difficult to confine family affairs to one or two appointed areas of the house. Many of us have grown accustomed to speaking our minds whenever we feel like it, regardless of where we may be. But think about it. Most families have definite rules about where in the house one can or cannot eat, or established areas for the children to play. Yet few of us create any rules for discussion of family matters and the day-to-day living arrangements within the home. We give even less attention to what we want our bedrooms to represent.

FROM THE TRENCHES
★★★★

*The club where I worked had 11 distinctly themed private V.I.P. rooms. Every room conjured up a different feel, yet there was one thing alike, the warm and inviting elemental mood created by us girls.*

The men who passed time with us in the V.I.P. rooms always felt completely welcomed. We catered to their natural desire to feel wanted and at peace. At the end of a long day's work, does your mate look forward to coming home? Will he find peace or aggravation? Does your husband feel welcomed and wanted in his own home, or does he feel like an intruder?

*There should be areas of your home which are only associated with delight. The bedroom is one of them.*

My mother was an excellent cook, and I still vividly remember the delicious smells that came from her kitchen. We had a hot breakfast almost every morning and a hot meal almost every night. Watching my mom prepare those meals are some of my fondest memories of childhood; they are also the reason my kids rarely get cold cereal or fast food in my home. I don't remember anything bad ever happening in my mother's kitchen; just lots of laughs over great food at the picnic-style table where we all sat. My mother's routine in the kitchen helped to create a wonderful memory of that space. To this day, when I visit my mother's home, we always end up sitting at the kitchen table.

## CREATE AN ISLAND OF PEACE

There should be areas of your home which are only associated with delight. The bedroom is one of them. If we can so easily build magical memories of a kitchen, imagine what you can do with your bedroom. Learn what ingredients you need to create a recipe of success in the bedroom area. You may want to start with recess lighting, plush pillows, serene color-schemes, scented candles, sensuous melodies, a cleaner environment, and no complaining. Your spouse should never be made to feel as if he is invading your space or that any area of the home or item in the home is more sacred and valuable than his peace and pleasure.

*Thoughts of a visit to the V.I.P. room fill our male patrons with pleasure immediately.*

Thoughts of a visit to the V.I.P. room fill our male patrons with pleasure immediately. They know they're heading for a safe haven instead of a battle zone. It's normal to flee from pain and embrace pleasure. At the very least, your marriage bed should not be defiled by harsh words, which are not conducive to a peaceful, romantic setting. If you consistently nag or argue in the bedroom area, then before long, only negative feelings will be attached to that space. Your man won't run to refuge in your bedroom; he'll only retreat.

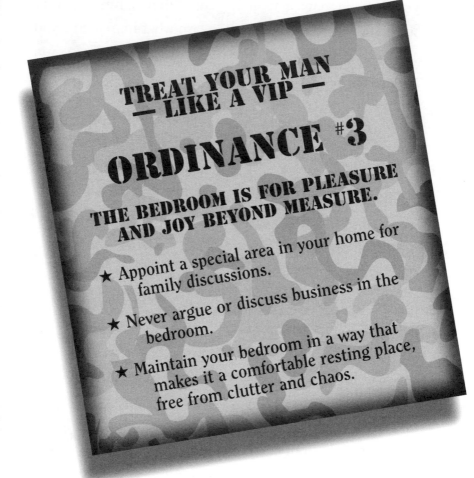

TREAT YOUR MAN
— LIKE A VIP —

# ORDINANCE #3

## THE BEDROOM IS FOR PLEASURE AND JOY BEYOND MEASURE.

★ Appoint a special area in your home for family discussions.

★ Never argue or discuss business in the bedroom.

★ Maintain your bedroom in a way that makes it a comfortable resting place, free from clutter and chaos.

# Chapter 4
# SIR, YES SIR
*Uncommon communication*

One very slow night I was having a hard time selling a table dance, let alone an invitation to a private V.I.P. room. Every customer in the house seemed unnaturally frugal. I noticed one gentleman sitting alone in the corner toward the back of the room.

"It's time to get my hustle on," I commented to the girl on the bar stool next to mine.

"He's cheap. Doesn't spend money on table dances. Says he'll only buy a girl a drink," she replied.

Despite this tidbit of information, I strutted over anyway. As I sat down the gentleman exclaimed, "I'll buy you a drink Honey, but I never spend money on dances."

*Trying to persuade the customer he was wrong would have annoyed him and put him on the defensive.*

To which I replied, "Double shot of Maker's on the rocks for me."

Now, the same man had made exactly the same statement to two distinctly different individuals. The difference between me and the girl on the barstool was that I did not limit the menu to table dances and V.I.P. rooms. I was willing to investigate what the client did want instead of concentrating on what he didn't.

As the evening wore on we talked about art, poetry, theatre—any topic for which we shared a fondness. At one point in the conversation he declared, "The arts are definitely something I liberally spend money on." So while it's true I did not receive one penny from that customer for dances, I did earn several hundred dollars for recitations of Poe, Frost, Shakespeare and my favorite female poet, Nikki Giovanni. I had decided early on I would not waste time and energy trying to change the customer's mind about the unparalleled joy that could be found in the purchase of one of my fabulous table dances. Neither would I explain why his purchase of a drink did not add to my bottom line. Trying to persuade the customer he was wrong would have annoyed him and put him on the defensive. Instead, by respecting his decision, I made it easier for him to open up.

*Women tend to speculate about what was NOT said instead of hearing what was.*

## YOU DON'T HAVE TO AGREE

People are more forthright if you value their opinions; you don't have to agree to appreciate their line of thinking. Instead of forcing my will on the client, I patiently uncovered his interest — the arts — and then proceeded to lavish him with enthusiasm. It was a win/win situation: he got the wonderful treat of unexpected poetry, and I got the unexpected opportunity to make money with my clothes on.

*Working at the club I spent a lot of time with men. I studied them, learned from them, and learned to hear as they hear. Hearing the way a man hears means using logic—not emotions—to process what's being said. The patron in the club that evening made two declarations: I will buy you a drink, and I don't spend money on table dances. He didn't say he didn't have money; he just said he wouldn't spend it on table dances.*

Women tend to speculate about what was not said instead of hearing what was. In the battle of effective communication this is the wrong defense. If you are guilty of this practice, you may be causing your relationship considerable harm. Try not to add or detract from your mate's comments, and your ability to hear and understand him will increase. If you are unclear about his meaning, ask him. Do not make assumptions based on limited details or accusations based on an active imagination. Listen to the facts. Review the facts. Accept the facts. Respond based on the facts. Although it will take effort to use logic instead of emotion when communicating, the rewards are well worth it.

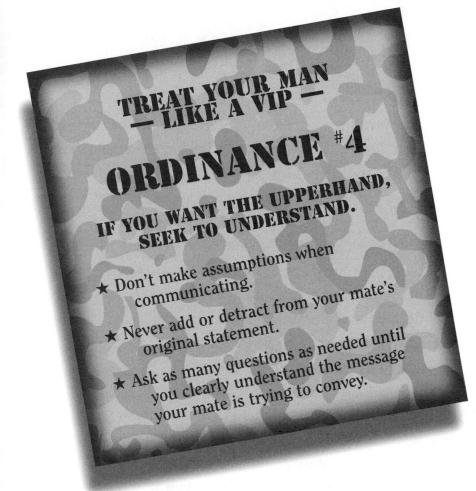

TREAT YOUR MAN
— LIKE A VIP —

# ORDINANCE #4

## IF YOU WANT THE UPPERHAND, SEEK TO UNDERSTAND.

★ Don't make assumptions when communicating.

★ Never add or detract from your mate's original statement.

★ Ask as many questions as needed until you clearly understand the message your mate is trying to convey.

## Chapter 5
# DAILY REVEILLE
*Take control of your environment*

I perform a ritual every morning before I wake my kids for school. The goal is to take control of my environment and to create an atmosphere of peace that will follow them for the rest of the day. I have no idea what will happen once they leave home; I can only do what is in my control. I turn on one of their favorite CDs; and as the music plays, I wake them up one by one. I time everything so that each one can have some time alone in the bath-

*Does your husband enjoy the prospect of getting out of bed and starting another day with you?*

room. Waking them up ten minutes apart is a simple solution to quell what could easily develop into unnecessary confusion. I hate arguing in the morning; the ten-minute separation helps to make my kids' morning, and my morning, peaceful and serene regardless of what the rest of the day may bring.

Analyze your daily routine. What is your customary mood in the morning? Do you find yourself rushing because of something you did not do the night before? Does your day begin with disorganization or is your household running like a well constructed device? Does your chaos dominate the atmosphere in your home? Is your husband late because you can't find little Jimmy's socks or forgot to check Mary's homework the night before?

## SAVE THE DRAMA

Unnecessary drama can be avoided with better organization. For example, a friend of mine checks her kids' homework while driving them to school. What was once a last-minute fix has evolved into a daily routine. Though she's actually one of the kindest, most compassionate people I know, she is endangering the life of every one on the road because she can't manage to check her kids' homework at night. She has a routine, but it's neither safe, nor effective, nor positive. Instead, her routine is rooted in chaos, crisis, and confusion.

Is there peace inside your home most mornings? Have you put thought into creating a consistent atmosphere of tranquility for your spouse and your family? Does your husband enjoy the prospect of getting out of bed and starting another day with you? If the answer to any of these questions is "no," get busy.

There are many tools available to help you get organized. Start with a day planner. If you spend a lot of your time on the computer you may want to use its calendar feature, as well. I'm a personal fan of the Post-It and you can find them on the dashboard of my car at any given time. If I switch purses and forget my planner, or if I don't use my computer on a particular day, the Post-Its serve as a dependable back up. Rarely does a day go by that I don't drive my car.

Make a list of the chores you perform on a regular basis. If you are ironing in the morning, perhaps you should iron at night. If you are ironing daily, perhaps you should iron for the week. Maybe it's time to teach the kids to iron; knowing how to delegate responsibility is a part of getting organized. Everyone in the family should have some sort of house hold chore. Even a five year old can wipe the kitchen table, place laundry in a hamper, or put biscuits in the doggie bowl. Every morning when you arise, take the offensive. Methodically execute your plan of attack to prevent most uprisings and help keep your home orderly, harmonious and hostility free.

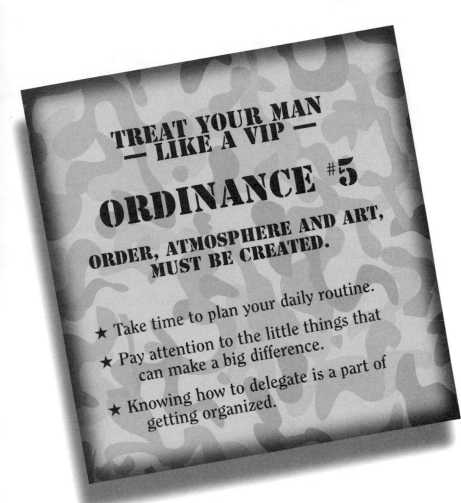

TREAT YOUR MAN
— LIKE A VIP —

# ORDINANCE #5

## ORDER, ATMOSPHERE AND ART, MUST BE CREATED.

★ Take time to plan your daily routine.

★ Pay attention to the little things that can make a big difference.

★ Knowing how to delegate is a part of getting organized.

*Chapter 6*
# THE BATTLE LINES HAVE BEEN DRAWN
*How to work what you've got*

"The eye eats first," is the slogan that a seasoned dancer lives by. First comes the customer's attraction; then, the desire to possess. You can never arrive at stage two without going through stage one. Despite the blonde hair, blue-eyed myth, different men are attracted to different things. This realization came as a devastating blow to some dancers who took every rejection as a personal indictment. Eventually, those girls left the business with their self-esteem destroyed.

*Never compete on an uneven playing field, especially if you're out-cupped.*

Successful sales people know their product, and they also know their client-base. How well do you know yourself? What do you consider to be your best physical attribute? What do you consider to be your best character attribute? How do you play up these attributes? What are your greatest flaws? Does the man in your life you seek to please share your opinion about yourself? If not, what does his list consist of? Do you have secrets for hiding your flaws?

I have natural breasts — a "B" cup, which is average. Often while working I would notice the dancers who had implants intimidating the smaller, natural-breasted performers. The natural-breasted dancers would then pass negative comments about the implants, which magnified their own insecurities enormously. Though at times I have felt threatened by mammoth boobs, I never made the mistake of competing against a girl who possessed double "D" implants for a man who is obviously mesmerized by big breasts. Never compete on an uneven playing field, especially if you're out-cupped.

I knew that my two greatest features were my eyes and my back. Though these two features may sound hard to peddle against saline and silicone, I understood my job was to convince a client it was much more fulfilling to drown in the depths of my eyes than to smother in a pair of those augmented breasts. It worked—many times.

## KEEP IT REAL

You will not exude confidence if you are trying to be something you are not. Women should never define themselves by the latest trends in fashion magazines. If advertisers market women with big breasts, we feel compelled to get implants. If advertisers market women who are thin, we all want to lose extreme amounts of weight. As fashion and movie industries thrust ever-changing standards of "beauty" upon us, we feel obliged to conform, even if these images are unnatural or unrealistic. Men do not keep up with the latest fashion trends. I can attest from my own experiences inside the club no one has informed the men adoring a full figure that it is no longer en vogue.

This is not an endorsement to be overweight. Your ultimate goal whether size 6 or 16 should be the best physical condition possible that will facilitate a life of fewer health complications. I cannot think of anything more miserable than trying to convert yourself into something you are not, or trying to fit into a mold you're not genetically predisposed to fit. It takes much less energy to be you than it does to try and imitate someone else. Being you can be both fulfilling and rewarding, but first you must determine who you are. Never allow others to define you.

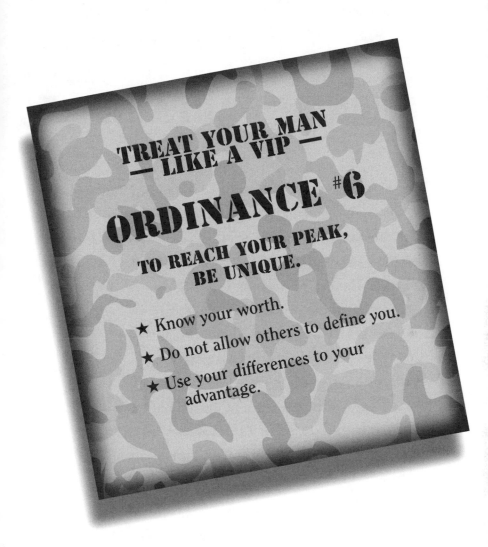

TREAT YOUR MAN
— LIKE A VIP —

# ORDINANCE #6

TO REACH YOUR PEAK,
BE UNIQUE.

★ Know your worth.
★ Do not allow others to define you.
★ Use your differences to your
advantage.

## Chapter 7
# TRENCH WARFARE
*Managing your feminine assets*

In the club, we women celebrated our physical differences from the men. We flaunted our femininity and wielded our womanly wiles; they in turn saluted our softness and clapped for our curves. Generally, women are more fragile than men (although physical differences have no correlation to intellectual equality or decision-making skills). Here, in the world of skin and sensuality, we know we are unlike men; and we ruthlessly use it to our advantage. We've got it. We work it, and they want it. Why should it be any different between you and your mate?

> *We've got it. We work it, and they want it.*

Remember the "Look what I have..." or "You show me yours; I'll show you mine," phase from second grade, when you realized little boys had things little girls did not? Compare-and-contrast was the name of the game, and each person's differences were a source of intrigue and adventure. Flash forward to today.

> *When men enter the club they immediately recognize that gender lines are not blurred. This separation of the sexes remind the men of simpler times, when boys were boys and girls were girls, and everyone took pride in being as God created them.*

## GIRL POWER

If you are a working wife, your femininity may not be an asset at your place of employment, but it should be inside your home. Stop competing at home like you do at the office and put yourself in a less aggressive mode. Your husband should not come home from a hard day at work and find he is married to one of "the guys." If you have gradually evolved into a masculine version of your former self over the years, you must quickly reverse this process. Do whatever is within your power to eliminate this unappealing façade: change your hair, schedule a professional makeover, buy sensuous apparel, wear high heels, adopt an

*Accentuate and celebrate all of your gender differences.*

approachable attitude, put on a smile. You and your spouse are allies—not competitors and not physical equals. Accentuate and celebrate all of your gender differences. This does not mean you should transform into some helpless creature; it means your husband should not think of you and "the guys" interchangeably.

If you are a stay at home mom, this is no excuse to become haggard and matronly. You must carefully balance your role as mother and spouse. Your husband may have married you because you have wonderful qualities akin to his mom, but your primary role is that of wife. Before you became the mother of his kids, you were the sensuous lover he couldn't resist, the one who captured his heart, aroused his loins and inspired him to pledge a vow unto death.

Are you still the WOMAN your husband fell in love with, or have you become some androgynous creature with whom he now shares space? P.M.S. should not be the only sign there is a female in the house.

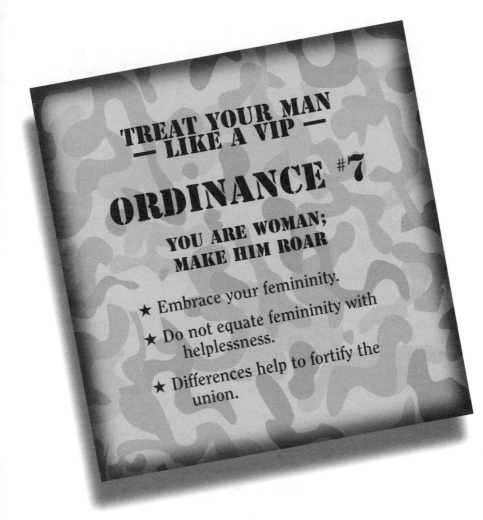

## TREAT YOUR MAN — LIKE A VIP —

## ORDINANCE #7

### YOU ARE WOMAN; MAKE HIM ROAR

★ Embrace your femininity.

★ Do not equate femininity with helplessness.

★ Differences help to fortify the union.

# Chapter 8
# RESTORE OR RETIRE
### Digging beneath the surface

Assuming your relationship is long-term, you have spent a considerable amount of time with your mate and know things about him that can only be discerned over time, things a stripper could never learn. You and your mate have a unique history that cannot be replicated by anyone else. Instead of thinking of your relationship with your mate as something to retire, envision it as something to restore. Underneath the build-up of disappointment, frustration and monotony lies a hidden treasure waiting to be stripped down and exposed. Both you and your relationship are a classic; you are valuable, beautiful and rare.

*Do not make plans to transform your mate. The revolution starts within...*

Have you ever witnessed a man working to restore an automobile that sparked memories of his youth? The more the project develops, the more obsessed he becomes: preening over every detail, trying to recapture a pleasurable moment in time. Considering that there have been many joyful moments in your relationship and you have established a good foundation on which to build, ask yourself what you can do to restore your relationship to its former glory, or better still, something greater.

## SELF-REFORM

Do not make plans to transform your mate. The revolution starts within; the transformation must be to yourself and your attitude. Take stock of how you have changed over the years. Make a list of the changes and decide if they have negatively or positively impacted the relationship.

Have you ever taken a special moment to dress or undress for your man?

*In the club, I spent a lot of time getting dressed and undressed for men; and they were enthralled with even the slightest detail. It always amazed me. They were intrigued by something as minor as a toe ring, piercing or an interesting hairstyle they had never seen before. I once spent fifteen minutes in a V.I.P. room explaining how I curl my hair with drinking straws. The men noticed eye makeup, nail dressings, and the firmness or softness of skin.*

Because they were conditioned to certain images of their wives, any deviations from these images were met with great interest.

Since the atmosphere inside your home is so familiar, the adjustments you make may need to be major in order to have a similar impact. Drop a dress size or two. Consult your dermatologist about micro-dermabrasion treatments. Adopt a less contentious attitude around the house. Plan family meals a week in advance. Choose to speak positively about your relationship at all times. Consistently set aside quality time to spend with your spouse. Do not expect your husband to notice the small adjustments at the onset. As you continue with the restoration project and significant results are noticeable, it will appear as though you have enacted changes all at once. Be persistent; he will notice!

*A happier, healthier you will make a more interesting and favorable partner.*

Because the plan you create involves changes to you alone, it should also include the cultivation of some personal aspirations. It is as important to work diligently toward emotional restoration as it is to restore yourself physically. Perhaps you may enjoy photography courses, dance classes, volunteer work, or a degree of higher learning that has eluded you thus far. Get involved in something that contributes to your development without causing conflict in your relationship. A happier, healthier you will make a more interesting and favorable partner. A woman with no personal ambition is as unappetizing and unappealing as a man with no purpose.

Take inventory to determine where the problems lie. Are you aging like fine wine, or do you look in the mirror and start to whine? Are you as positive, involved and supportive as you once were? Are you and your spouse living two separate lives under the same roof? Perhaps you are exactly the opposite, smothering your mate because you no longer have any ambitions of your own, trying desperately to enjoy life vicariously through him. You may not be pleased with all the answers to these piercing questions. If you are dissatisfied, I suspect your mate may be equally dissatisfied. Nevertheless, with consistent effort, your relationship can be revived. Create and implement a restoration plan that will allow you to become the classic you were destined to be — the irreplaceable, involved, interesting, well-groomed, loving wife of his youth.

# TREAT YOUR MAN — LIKE A VIP —

## ORDINANCE #8

### NOTHING IS MORE CHIC THAN A RARE ANTIQUE.

★ Mature in a way that increases your value.

★ Periodically take inventory of how changes in you are affecting the relationship.

★ You're never too old to set new goals.

## Chapter 9
# OUTRANKED
*Follow the leader*

If you were reared in a single parent household where your mother led the troops, your idea of family hierarchy might be a little distorted. Because your mother was the sole provider or primary caregiver, necessity not choice caused her to emerge as the family's main decision maker. Fortunately, you have choices your mother did not; and your choice to relinquish authority may be vital to your relationship's success. This is not a novel concept, nor should it be considered archaic. The notion of order in relationships is practical and contemporary. You must adopt this concept of a designated order within your marriage and be ruthless in your execution.

FROM THE TRENCHES
★ ★ ★ ★

*At the club there was an unspoken rule that the patrons were in charge unless otherwise indicated. Our goal was their pleasure, and all final decisions were up to them. Because we entrusted the men with the responsibility of determining the evening's excitement, they never felt vulnerable because of lack of expertise.*

35

In our care, a topless bar novice would still be made to feel like a worldly renaissance man and was more than willing to succumb to our delicate touch. We never threatened their masculinity. We conducted ourselves as the Ready Reserve, meaning we remained reserved until they were ready.

## FILE FOLDERS

Think of your marriage as a computer. The modern world is filled with inventions labeled as time-efficient, cost-efficient, or energy-efficient, with the ultimate goal of maximum functionality. Until now, you have been operating as the mainframe of this computer. When the mainframe begins to run out of storage space, previous information must be archived to make room for new material. It is easy to forget the information stored in the archive files as your use of this material gradually diminishes. Perhaps you have stored away some important files that are critical to the success of your marriage. Contained in these files might be your sensuality, sense of humor, or the sense of style that separated

*We conducted ourselves as the Ready Reserve, meaning we remained reserved until they were ready.*

you from all the other women in your husband's life and made you the one he chose to marry. Access these files and use them to your advantage.

You are the auxiliary unit, the reserve, and an elite special force to be used when his own strength and wisdom are not enough. You must now transition and liberate yourself from a role you were never intended by nature to play. By relinquishing your role as the mainframe to your mate, you will position yourself as an asset that continuously increases in value.

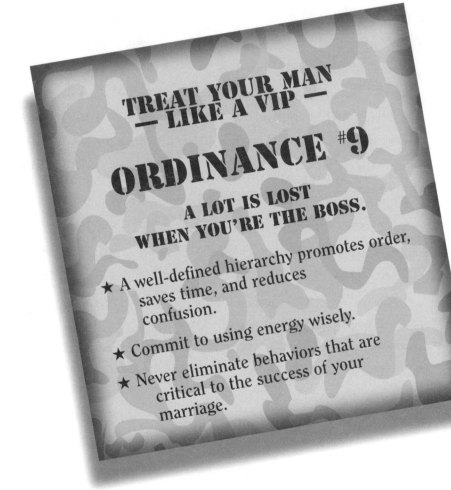

TREAT YOUR MAN
— LIKE A VIP —

# ORDINANCE #9

## A LOT IS LOST
## WHEN YOU'RE THE BOSS.

★ A well-defined hierarchy promotes order, saves time, and reduces confusion.

★ Commit to using energy wisely.

★ Never eliminate behaviors that are critical to the success of your marriage.

# Chapter 10
# KP DUTY
Secrets, sex and sauces

With the success of such movies as *9 ½ Weeks, Like Water For Chocolate,* and *Chocolat,* the eroticism of food has become apparent. As a New Orleans native, I understand food itself to be anything but simple. Kahlil Gibran wrote, "Your most savory meal is that which you eat at the other person's table." My body still rises past its boiling point as I recall my most savory dessert. I was dating a man whose passion for food I assumed was similar to my own. We mainly dined out, or I personally prepared the few home-cooked meals we enjoyed together. One of my favorite desserts is a good brownie with lots of pecans. After observing my brownie

*Think of every meal as an opportunity to make love to your spouse's palette...*

addiction for a few months, my gentleman suitor informed me of a secret recipe he had acquired and offered to bake me the most delicious brownies I ever tasted. I accepted his invitation, though I decided beforehand not to allow my expectations to get the best of me.

As he shopped for the ingredients and began to prepare what he claimed would be his "masterpiece," I peacefully napped upon the couch in his French Quarter suite. His warm breath upon my cheek eventually stirred me along with the gentle nudge of his hand. I awakened from my slumber to see that the lights were dimmed, candles were burning and on the table sat two saucers with steaming hot brownies and two cups of fresh brewed coffee. I was carried to the table and placed into a chair in front of one of the delicious servings. He was right! The brownies were exquisite, but they paled in comparison to what happened next.

## QUIZ SHOW

After an invitation to do so, I was unsuccessful in guessing the secret ingredient, which consisted of some sort of liqueur. We decided I should try the unused brownie mix to assist me in my plight. I licked the spoon several times but to no avail. He seemed pretty smug about the way the events were unfolding and was a little surprised I was having trouble with naming the alcohol based ingredient. In a moment of playfulness, I dipped my hand inside the bowl saturating my fingers with the gooey mixture. It felt moist and cold. My dripping hand landed softly on his left cheek. His long fingers quickly sank into the bowl. Suddenly a batter fight ensued. In the end we were each covered with brownie mix wherever flesh was exposed. It took hours to lick the brownie mix off each other's bodies. And yes, along with everything else that night, the secret ingredient was revealed.

If you think of every meal as an opportunity to make love to your spouse's palette, something as routine as lunch or dinner preparation can evolve into an orgasmic symphony of the taste buds or maybe even an orgasm itself.

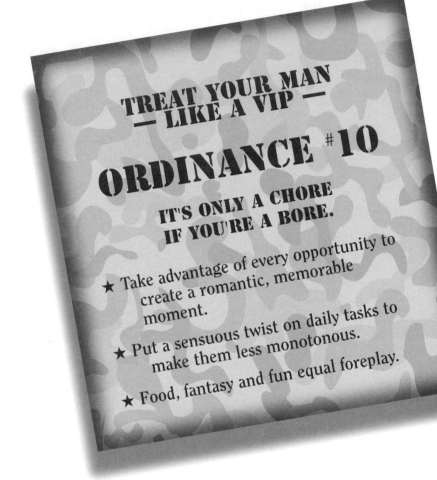

TREAT YOUR MAN
— LIKE A VIP —

# ORDINANCE #10

## IT'S ONLY A CHORE IF YOU'RE A BORE.

★ Take advantage of every opportunity to create a romantic, memorable moment.

★ Put a sensuous twist on daily tasks to make them less monotonous.

★ Food, fantasy and fun equal foreplay.

*Chapter 11*
# DEFINING THE MISSION
*Plan your reaction*

One of my girlfriends told me, "My husband and I are no longer 'growing' in the same direction." The notion of her husband 'growing' in her direction seemed odd when I considered how nature develops. There is a planting season, a watering season, and a reaping season. It is not likely you and your mate can coordinate these stages in the same areas throughout your lives, since "growth" can be spontaneous. The key to a successful marriage is not "growing" in his direction, but "going" in his direction, which is a matter of choice and an act of will. If you and your family have been functioning without established objectives, you must come together to create a concise set of goals for your family unit and institute a plan of action to achieve these goals. There must be goals implemented that will benefit the unit as a whole.

> *An individual goal should never undermine or take precedence over a mutual goal.*

Start your family's goal with a mission statement. The goals you identify should line up with your family's mission. Don't make abstract statements. You and your mate may have different interpretations of a goal if it is not well defined, and this may cause confusion at some later date. Designate each person's role and responsibility in helping to achieve each goal. Some goals may be the sole responsibility of one partner. A stay-at-home wife may not contribute to family finances, but she can ensure an efficient household. Decide as a couple which skills and talents will better serve your unit. Create a visible checklist of everyone's responsibilities. The checklist is not a tool for finger pointing, but a guide to track progress and make adjustments as needed.

*To be ALL good means your actions and intentions are good all the time.*

When a crisis arises, counteract negative behavior with positive action until the source of the problem can be determined and harmony restored. Do not make permanent decisions under pressure when a viable temporary solution may be found in the interim.

Perhaps your husband has a new boss who is making his life at work miserable, and a task he once easily performed at home has now become burdensome. This is not the time to attack him for lack of performance, but rather an opportunity for Special Forces to kick in. You could make a temporary adjustment and perform his task until his season of frustration at work has ended.

## GET PERSONAL

After you have completed a list of goals for your family, complete a list of personal goals for yourself. This will eliminate the tendency we have as women to consume ourselves with our mates and families without saving a little for ourselves. You must determine beforehand that your plans for the union are ALL good. This means an individual goal should never undermine or take precedence over a mutual goal. If you are creating goals for yourself that weaken the family unit, then your plans for the union are not ALL good. If your response toward your husband is tit-for-tat, then your plans for the union are not ALL good. To be ALL good means your actions and intentions are good all the time.

This also implies that when your mate's actions are less than honorable, the quality of your commitment should not be affected. Your vows are not based on his performance, but on your integrity. If your husband's selfish behavior is weakening the family unit, similar behavior from you will only accelerate the demise. It is normal for unplanned family problems to arise. Your reaction to each problem will determine if your relationship survives. Your marriage is a living, breathing organism. It is alive. If you envision your marriage as dead or dying, it won't take long before you bury it.

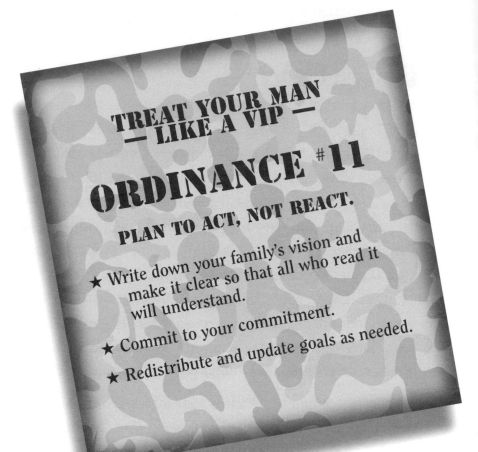

## TREAT YOUR MAN — LIKE A VIP —

# ORDINANCE #11

### PLAN TO ACT, NOT REACT.

★ Write down your family's vision and make it clear so that all who read it will understand.

★ Commit to your commitment.

★ Redistribute and update goals as needed.

Chapter 12
# REDEFINING THE MISSION
*Keeping pace with evolution*

I remember meeting several men at the club who were starting new businesses. Their anticipation and excitement was comparable to that of an expectant mother. After all, who begins a new endeavor without a certain degree of optimism? While I was happy to participate in the customer's jubilation, I understood that a seed that takes root must go through several transformations before it produces any fruit. Their business aspirations were no different. The ability to recognize these stages of development or seasons as I referred to earlier will benefit your relationship. Because change is constant, identifying a season before it takes place will enable you to prepare and respond accordingly.

> *The time and manner in which advice is given helps to determine how well it is received.*

Each season comes with a completely different set of traits as it pertains to your mate's personality. Each season has its own demands. Let's use the new business owners as an example. These gentlemen have progressed through all three stages of planting, sowing, and reaping. They've completed their first evolution by progressing from potential entrepreneurs to owning their own businesses. Now, they are in the planting stages again; this time their goals are to make the new businesses success-ful. They must water the seeds accordingly if their businesses are

*As your family evolves and expands, so will your responsibilities.*

to survive and thrive. The fruit of this new season is a flour-ishing company. Starting a business is an accomplishment in itself, but making it successful involves a greater level of commitment and determination. The same is true with your marriage. As your family evolves and expands, so will your responsibilities.

Because these men were in their planting stages, a time marked by expectation and celebration, it was effortless for me to lift my champagne glass and offer them a heartfelt toast. Their behaviors and attitudes were characteristic of their stage of development. Any words of stripper wisdom at that moment would have been unfruitful.

## THE WINDOW OF OPPORTUNITY

There is an appropriate moment to offer advice that might be beneficial to your mate. The time and manner in which advice is given helps to determine how well it is received. Unsolicited yet valuable counsel is best served warm, not hot; this means you should offer your opinion in a loving, non-hostile environment.

Learn to recognize a change in seasons before it happens. Expect change. Study your mate's response as he endures each season, and then develop a plan of action on how to make each transition occur as smoothly for your family as is within your power. Be aware of your limitations. There will always be factors you can't control whenever change occurs. Evolution is continuous, so don't fight the process.

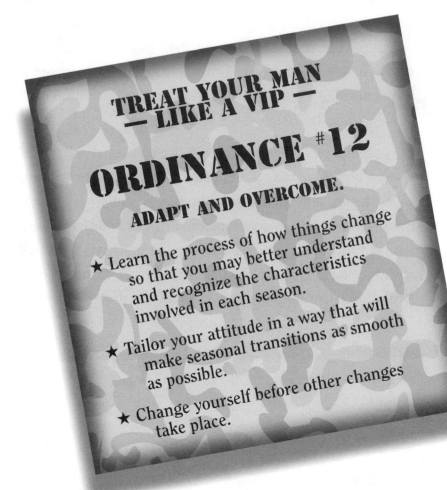

TREAT YOUR MAN
— LIKE A VIP —

# ORDINANCE #12

## ADAPT AND OVERCOME.

★ Learn the process of how things change so that you may better understand and recognize the characteristics involved in each season.

★ Tailor your attitude in a way that will make seasonal transitions as smooth as possible.

★ Change yourself before other changes take place.

## Chapter 13
# ALLIES
# OR ADVERSARIES
Successful systems of support

I was having a slow night, so I performed my "I'm having a bad night" ritual poem, by Nikki Giovanni—"Ego Tripping" to myself in the mirror of the ladies' bathroom. As always, it helped me regain my confidence, and I decided to circulate the room once more. Another girl's Sugar Daddy entered the club. Fortunately, the girl and I were friends, and I had joined them for drinks and table dances in the past. "X, over here. Pete will buy you a drink. Right, Pete?"

*Befriending someone in a church setting is not a valid reason to suspend sound judgment.*

"Whatever you want," Pete replied. "Name the evening's poison."

Pete motioned for his waitress and I ordered my usual. "Double shot of Maker's on the rocks, please."

After extended conversation, my girlfriend and I performed a few rounds of table dances for Pete. As was his custom, Pete invited my girlfriend into the V.I.P. room for the rest of the evening. "Would you mind having two girls tonight?" she asked.

"She's an absolute doll. If you want her to come along it's fine with me. She's more than welcome," he said.

Pete spent three hours in the V.I.P. room that night. I stayed around for one. I knew it was best that I should run out before Pete's generosity did.

**FROM THE TRENCHES**
★ ★ ★ ★

*My friend's invitation that night grew out of a system of support we created that enabled us to make money together when one of us was having a bad night. The system of sharing a Sugar Daddy did not include all of the girls. It involved only about four of us who started performing at the club around the same time, and the system relied heavily on trust. We were all confident no one within our group would try to usurp the Sugar Daddy. The threat of a coup is why you don't share some things with individuals who have yet to establish credibility within your realm of ethics.*

## ACCESS DENIED

Consider the intimate details of your relationship with your spouse top-secret. Only people with a high-level security clearance qualify as confidants and supporters. It is never wise to discuss your lack of marital bliss with anyone with whom you have not established an extensive history unless they are a member of the clergy or a licensed therapist. The women you meet at church are no exception to this rule. Befriending someone in a church setting is not a valid reason to suspend sound judgment. Though their intentions may be honorable at the onset, anyone can be subject to temptation if given enough ammunition and opportunity.

*Respect the views of others, but trust yourself.*

Never solicit counsel from a disgruntled supporter. If your favorite confidant is having marital problems of her own, she may offer tainted advice. Try to find someone who is content with his or her spouse. Seeking the advice of someone who has already overcome a problem similar to the one you are experiencing with your mate will also be useful. Search for an older, mature couple that can mentor you through your current and future difficulties. Seek out positive supporters who can provide encouragement, allies who can nimbly shore up marital foundations and who understand the benefits of the restorative process.

Unless you are in a physically abusive relationship, the advice you receive from your supporters should benefit the unit as a whole and not only you as an individual. Be wary of bias in any counsel you obtain. Your friends can love you without loving your spouse. Reconsider any advice that does not work to the advantage of the unit as a whole. If the advice creates a further wedge in your relationship, find a new strategy immediately. It is hard to maintain hope in the restorative process when you are employing techniques that are ineffective.

*The only person who needs to believe in what you're fighting for is you.*

Fear or embarrassment should not prevent you from obtaining information about resources that may help to ensure the success of your marriage. There is no new thing under the sun. Someone has already been in your predicament and has published a book, recorded a tape, or released a video on the subject.

Only you know the inner workings of your marriage. This makes you qualified to be its staunchest advocate. Respect the views of others, but trust yourself. Any decisions you make need not be based on popular opinion. The only person who needs to believe in what you're fighting for is you.

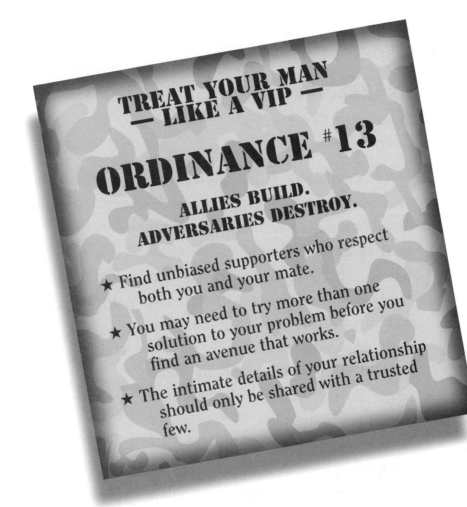

### TREAT YOUR MAN — LIKE A VIP —

# ORDINANCE #13

## ALLIES BUILD.
## ADVERSARIES DESTROY.

★ Find unbiased supporters who respect both you and your mate.

★ You may need to try more than one solution to your problem before you find an avenue that works.

★ The intimate details of your relationship should only be shared with a trusted few.

# Chapter 14
# MORSE CODE
Consistency is the key to clarity

Communication is the mortar that keeps relationships attached. Most relationships require both verbal and non-verbal communication, but your verbal and non-verbal cues must be congruent. Sending out mixed signals will create confusion that can paralyze any relationship. Don't say, "yes" if you mean "no." Say "no." You must ponder your actions, as well as your intentions, on a daily basis. Some people do not consider whether their actions are in line with the beliefs they so freely espouse, and the lack of daily deliberate action creates questions of trust. Plan how you will utilize each day. Only proceed with dealings that are consistent with who you would like to be as a person, parent, and mate. Are your actions consistent with the promises you have made to your spouse and family? Are your actions consistent with

*For your relationship to be successful you must define your role and conduct yourself in a manner consistent with that role.*

your spiritual and political beliefs? Are your actions benefiting you, your family, and the community in which you live? The answer to all these questions should be "yes."

## ISSUES OF TRUST

For your relationship to be successful you must define your role and conduct yourself in a manner consistent with that role. Your husband should never be left guessing if your word can be trusted. Your honor and integrity should not be sporadic or on a case-by-case basis. The more

*Remember your words have power if communication is to be your bond.*

inconsistent you are in matters of integrity the more challenging communication in the relationship becomes. If you are given to telling lies, every word you utter will become suspect. Your mate is forced to guess when you are telling the truth. If you are not forthright and consistent in word and deed, the entire communication process becomes unduly burdensome for all parties involved. Eventually, communication will be kept to a minimum or shut down altogether.

Remember your words have power if communication is to be your bond. They have the power to heal, to build, and to destroy. Know when to talk and when to be silent. Don't suffer from the "Chicken Little Syndrome" and run around exclaiming that the sky is falling whenever something goes slightly wrong. If you become known for over-dramatizing situations, your mate may not respond to crisis at the appropriate time. Speak responsibly, listen actively, and love unconditionally.

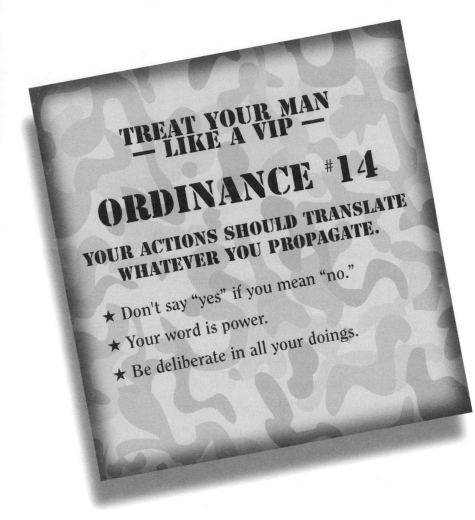

**TREAT YOUR MAN — LIKE A VIP —**

**ORDINANCE #14**

**YOUR ACTIONS SHOULD TRANSLATE WHATEVER YOU PROPAGATE.**

★ Don't say "yes" if you mean "no."

★ Your word is power.

★ Be deliberate in all your doings.

## Chapter 15
# EXPLORATION PARTY
*Pursue your pleasure past new limits*

No partner should be left sexually unfulfilled. This is a definite breach of the covenant relationship. The desire to mate is a natural biological function; therefore, sex should not be used as a tool of manipulation. Always think of love-making as an opportunity to meet a need in your mate's life that should never be met by someone else.

Forget any previous notion you may have had in the past that your husband's sexual fulfillment is not your responsibility. It is yours and yours alone. If you are no longer feeling passionate about your mate, try to develop a new attitude about your sex life. Adding variety might help increase interest. Most people have no desire to eat the same meal prepared in the same manner every day. This would surely be a recipe for boredom of the palette. Think of sex in the same way. If your standard routine in the bedroom has become so monotonous over the years that you no longer look forward to

*Focus your energy on pleasing him, and let his pleasure bring you the greatest joy.*

making love to your mate, you may need to consider new ideas to spice things up.

Commit to making your love life more exciting for your mate, especially if he is feeling equally unmotivated. Focus your energy on pleasing him, and let his pleasure bring you the greatest joy. Spend time pondering the sense of touch and all the gratification it encompasses. Make no early guesses based on your own likes and dislikes. A sexual position or soothing stroke that does not give pleasure to you may please your mate. Each individual must be explored on a case-by-case basis. There are areas of your mate's body that may respond to the simplest touch and other areas that may command a more authoritative approach. Don't assume that one rhythm will work for the duration.

*Teach him the tactical advantages of foreplay...*

## THE PLOT THICKENS

If you truly desire to arouse your mate's senses, think of his body as a book written in Braille that can only be translated by touch. As with any story there is a beginning a middle and end. There are highs and lows, crests and crescendos; and you must know them all. The more you read this book, the more familiar the story becomes; yet there will always be one detail or element that appears completely new. This book must become your favorite story, and no one else should know it more proficiently than you. For example, if you stroked your mate behind the knee, what would be his response? If you bit his inner thigh, nibbled his ankle, kissed his palm, sucked his elbow, or licked his brow, what then? Would he prefer a scalp massage or your recitation of prose?

If this sounds strange, I suspect you have been skipping the prologue and falling asleep on the epilogue of the book of "him." Instead of concentrating on the main story line, put some extra effort into sub-plots to spice things up. If you teach him the tactical advantages of foreplay, he will become not only a happy recipient, but also a proficient comrade in increasing your pleasure as well.

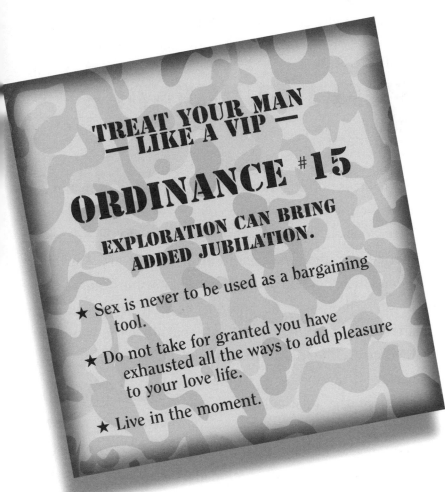

# TREAT YOUR MAN — LIKE A VIP —

# ORDINANCE #15

## EXPLORATION CAN BRING ADDED JUBILATION.

★ Sex is never to be used as a bargaining tool.

★ Do not take for granted you have exhausted all the ways to add pleasure to your love life.

★ Live in the moment.

# Chapter 16
# SWEET SURRENDER
*All defenses down*

There is nothing more debilitating to a relationship than resurrecting past hurts. Once you have closed old wounds, never reopen them. Forgiveness should be based not on merit but rather the condition of your heart. You either extend mercy or you don't. Most relationships cannot thrive in an atmosphere of unforgiveness; it will thwart any attempts at rebuilding your friendship with your mate. Relinquish the need to be right before it becomes a stumbling block in the relationship. If you must win every argument with your spouse, he will find it difficult to surrender to you emotionally. No one wants to be verbally battered into agreement. For your mate, it will become easier to resist sharing than to endure confrontation.

*Surrendering final decision-making power to your spouse is an issue of trust.*

When disagreements surface, present your case in the most humble way possible and allow him to make the final decisions. There can be no quorum in a democracy of two. Surrendering final decision-making power to your spouse is an issue of trust. You must trust him to have the best interest of the union at heart and to understand his own weaknesses and know your strengths. You do not need to expose his weaknesses to him; he will discover his flaws on his own. The daily demonstration of faith in your husband's decision-making skills will be added motivation for him to more carefully weigh each matter set before him. The more confident he becomes in his own decision-making abilities, the more comfortable he will become inquiring about and adhering to your advice. Build his confidence. It will contribute to your friendship. Do not tear him down, or he will not find it hard to allow a stranger to put back the pieces.

FROM THE TRENCHES
★ ★ ★ ★

*Most men I entertained inside the V.I.P. rooms of the club were not looking to have a sexual encounter; they were worldly enough to know men rarely score inside of topless bars. They wanted to be listened to, validated and encouraged. They were not deprived of sexual fulfillment as much as they craved the absence of judgment. Without realizing it, many clients were trying to make an emotional connection, and I could definitely relate.*

As exotic entertainers, we were frequently judged unfairly. The sympathy we extended to the customers developed out of our own desire for understanding and compassion.

## THE BUDDY SYSTEM

Your chances of subduing your mate physically are greatly diminished if you have not subdued him emotionally. The beautification process must start from within. Reignite his friendship and his flame will follow. One good friend is more precious than 100 great lovers, and

*Don't pray for peace inside your home; initiate it!*

you aspire to be both. The way your mate feels about his friendship with you will also influence whether you are making love or having sex. A degree of concern is involved in getting a woman to the point of orgasm. If your husband displays concern about your physical satisfaction, you are indeed making love. If he shows little concern for your sexual needs the friendship is eroding and must be rebuilt before you proceed.

Determine the role you desire to play in your relationship — friend or foe, builder or destroyer, lover or fighter — and submit to the characteristics that encompass that role. Forgive yourself for any previous shortcomings, and think of each new day as an opportunity to walk circumspectly in the role you have chosen to play. Do not concentrate on your husband's role or lack of performance. Check yourself. Don't pray for peace inside your home; initiate it! Take the lead in making your household the most serene place on the planet. The more peaceful the environment in your home, the more susceptible your husband will be to any changes you begin. Initiating physical changes in a hostile environment is futile. So, determine from this day forward that you will create an atmosphere of peace within your home by employing the tactic of sweet surrender. Surrender the need to be right. Surrender the desire to pass judgment. Surrender past hurts. Surrender pessimism. Surrender criticism. Surrender control.

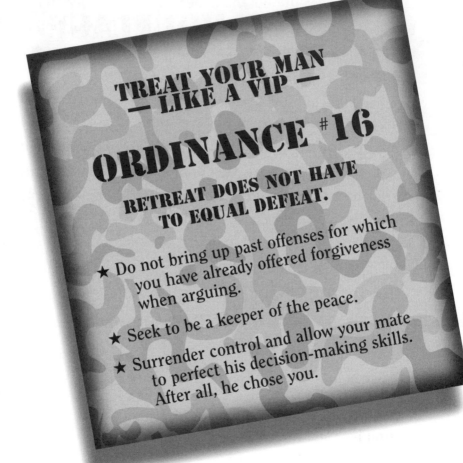

TREAT YOUR MAN
— LIKE A VIP —

# ORDINANCE #16

### RETREAT DOES NOT HAVE TO EQUAL DEFEAT.

★ Do not bring up past offenses for which you have already offered forgiveness when arguing.

★ Seek to be a keeper of the peace.

★ Surrender control and allow your mate to perfect his decision-making skills. After all, he chose you.

*Chapter 17*
# COVERT CAMOUFLAGE
*Beauty tricks of the trade*

## HAIR:

★ Every woman should own at least one wig and one wig piece. They will help to ensure you never have a bad hair day and add variety to your regular wardrobe. I suggest a wig piece the color of your hair and a wig that is the opposite extreme in hairstyle and color of your daily coiffure. If your hair is long, try something short. If your hair is red, try something blonde. Owning wigs and hairpieces presents you with a variety of options that are neither permanent nor damaging to your natural hair and can be invoked whenever the mood arises.

*Owning wigs and hairpieces presents you with a variety of options...*

★ Hair curlers worn to bed should be the exception, not the norm. The sight of curlers being worn to bed shocks many men because sleeping in curlers is a behavior most women never employ during the dating phase of their relationship. Waking up beautiful should be a priority both before and after the wedding. You can make exceptions for special occasions, but thirty years after the "I do" you should still go to bed in a dignified manner.

★ Pin curling the hair is a viable option to rollers. They are more comfortable for sleeping and can be fashioned into an attractive hairstyle.

★ Note: If you must go to bed wearing a scarf, I suggest you find several fashionable scarves that coordinate with your bedtime attire. Please tie it in a manner unlike a hairdo-rag.

*Learn to eat in a way that is healthy and enjoyable.*

## NAILS:

★ It is better to have no polish than chipped polish. Chipped polish takes away from a well-groomed appearance. If you do not like using a topcoat alone, and insist on colored polish, lighter colors are not as easily noticed as the darker colors when they are beginning to wear off.

★ A bottle of nail polish remover can also be used to remove hair dye from your hands and fingernails if you color your hair at home or use a rinse.

★ Nails don't need to be long, but they do need to be neat.

★ Keep an emery board in your purse for the occasional chipped nail.

## SKIN:

★ Baby oil in your bathwater will soften the areas that are unreachable. However, use a moisturizing wash for your face.

★ Regardless of skin tone, every woman can benefit from the use of sunscreen.

★ Cleanse, tone, and moisturize. Your face will be happier for it.

*Regardless of skin tone, every woman can benefit from the use of sunscreen.*

## FEET:

★ Toenails should be neatly clipped on a regular basis.

★ The same rules for nail polish apply for your toes.

★ Periodically rub petroleum jelly on your feet and cover them with thick cotton socks for several hours. Remove the socks and rub in any remaining petroleum jelly your skin has not absorbed.

★ Walking in bare feet causes them to callous faster. Wear shoes, socks, or slippers both indoors and out.

## BODY HAIR:

★ There are several options for the removal of unwanted body hair. Whether you choose tweezing, waxing or shaving, never leave home with a mustache, beard or untamed brows.

★ If you are uncomfortable about removing hair from your pubic area, there are professionals who are paid to perform this service. Less hair around the pubic area is aesthetically more appealing and cuts down on odors especially during the summer months.

## DIET:

★ Always consult a physician before starting any diet or exercise plan.

★ Learn to eat in a way that is healthy and enjoyable.

★ Find an exercise you can do every day with few limitations such as walking. All you need are walking shoes.

*Chapter 18*
# OPERATION SEDUCTION PRODUCTION

*Sensuous event planning*

## PROPS:

The two props I recommend are an armless chair and a pedestal if you are planning to perform table and lap dances at home. Owning a chair without any arms gives you a greater amount of flexibility such as straddling the chair while performing a dance for your man. The pedestal is your stage and will help to create a sense of excitement for you and your mate.

Sit your husband in an erect position in the armless chair and spread his legs apart. Once you have your husband properly seated, push the pedestal as close to the edge of the chair as possible. The two should be touching. Positioning your husband's legs spread eagle will enable you to have more space to perform. If you want to be face-to-face with your mate instead of towering over him on the pedestal, kneel on the portion of the chair that is exposed due to the spread eagle positioning of his legs, while placing your feet on the pedestal. Rest on your heels to be eye to eye. Kneel upright so that your breasts are at his eye level. Bending into this position at the onset puts you in nibbling range and may take away from the build-up. Use this move toward the middle or end if possible.

My standard procedure went as follows: I would place my hands on the customer's knees, lean in close, coyly smile, while gently spreading their legs and say, "Spread 'em, and I'm not the police." Then I pushed the pedestal against the edge of the chair and placed my hand out for assistance climbing on top of the

*A good performance should never feel like work and the mood should remain as festive as possible.*

pedestal. Holding their hand to get on the pedestal engages them from the onset and gives you support while you gain your balance and adjust to the surface of the pedestal. You can script your own movement and dialogue. Find an opening line that will lighten the mood for both you and your mate. A good performance should never feel like work and the mood should remain as festive as possible.

## SETTING:

My first visit to a jungle goes as follows: I arrived home one night from work and all of my plants were missing from my porch. At first, it looked like the work of the neighborhood drug addicts. I proceeded through the French doors of my home and found the inside lights were dimmed low. All of the furniture had been stripped from my living room area. Nothing remained but a sexy man in leopard print briefs lying on a mattress taken from a bed in another room, surrounded by beautiful plants. I had stepped into a jungle fantasy. Every plant both indoor and outdoor had been strategically placed throughout the room to create a jungle-like environment. My Tarzan awaited, and I had a marvelous time playing Jane.

*Some lights are easier on the thighs than others.*

As stated earlier in the book, order, atmosphere and art, must be created. Imagination, not money, is the key to creating romantic settings within your home. Pick a theme for your special night, and figure out what additional props you need to create the mood. Seeing my den converted into a nature scene made me want to swing from the ceiling fan!

## LIGHTING:

There are varieties of options when it comes to lighting. Some lights are easier on the thighs than others. The lights used when dancing on stage were blue, red, yellow and green. You can try colored lights to create a specific mood, or use a dimmer, or try candlelight or a fireplace instead. For the jungle scene within my home, lights were placed inside the clay pots of some of my plant holders. Instead of giving off full light, the pots only gave off shadows. The shadowy effect helped to give the jungle scene authenticity. Always be mindful of any fire hazards when working with lighting.

*A confident attitude will be the sexiest attire you can don when it comes to your intimate evenings.*

## MUSIC:

Because music contributes to the atmosphere, you should use tunes that ignite memories that are special to your relationship, as well as tunes you feel comfortable moving to. There is no written rule that the music must be slow. Choose a song that makes you and your mate feel good. When working in the club I would sometimes choose my music based on what conventions were in town. I tried to pick music that was familiar to most, like a Motown artist or something from the Rolling Stones.

I had two songs I danced to for my personal satisfaction. These were my signature songs. Some nights it was all about me, and I could care less about the crowd. Play your husband's favorite band, artist, composer, or song whenever the opportunity arises. If you are not comfortable dancing to his favorite tunes for a table dance, you may want to dance together as a couple as a prelude, and use your own music for the table dance itself.

## COSTUMES:

*Spend time learning your own body and do not be ashamed to convey what you learn.*

My number one suggestion is that you wear attire that is flattering to your shape and size and that makes you feel good about your appearance. You alone must determine this. Don't delude yourself in to thinking that sexy is only synonymous with a skimpy piece of lingerie. A confident attitude will be the sexiest attire you can don when it comes to your intimate evenings. You may want to choose attire that correlates with your theme if you've chosen one. My "Must Have" list consists of a pair of stiletto shoes, a garter belt, a pair of stockings, a long sleeve button down shirt, a necktie, a pair of cuff links and a fragrance. For me, these items are timeless classics, suitable for any body type or erotic occasion.

## DIRECTORIAL CUES:

Instructions are important. You can travel several routes to end up at the same destination, yet some routes are more scenic and interesting than others. Have your goals clearly defined and be able to communicate them to your mate. Some women feel uncomfortable discussing their sexual desires with their mate. Unfortunately, men are not mind readers. What works when making love to one may not work for another. You are putting your mate at a disadvantage if you are forcing him to rely solely on his previous experience as a lover. You are unique and may have special needs of which he is not aware.

*Never give a puppy a new bone and expect it to feign lack of interest.*

I like everything excessively slow. It's not likely any man would guess that if left to his own devices. I spent my entire college years without an orgasm because I was unaware of this important detail. Discovering a rhythm I enjoyed while lovemaking was a product of trial and error. Whenever my friends would talk about sex in college I thought they were exaggerating. My standard comment after a passionate night of lovemaking was "There has to be more to it than this." I never believed I could not orgasm, though I had been told that many times by my peers. I decided everyone's love making techniques were amiss. I was right!

Spend time learning your own body and do not be ashamed to convey what you learn. If you are anticipating a clitoral and vaginal orgasm, tell your spouse. Know if you would enjoy them separately or simultaneously, and then sketch out the path he should take to achieve the desired result. Without input from you, some men will never arrive at your desired sexual destination. Don't assume your husband knows what you want or a better way to get there. If he is not accustomed to receiving verbal directives from you, write them down as a map and turn it into a game. Give him a mental image of what the results are going to be. Men love a worthwhile objective. Compass anyone?

## SPECIAL EFFECTS (SFX):

Some of the methods you enact to rekindle your love life may fall outside of your comfort zone. Only you and your mate can determine where to draw the line. I do not suggest the addition of a third party as an option to improving your love life. The benefits never outweigh the negatives. Every couple I entertained in a private room (except one) ended in complete disaster. Some did not make it past the first table dance. What started off as a fun adventure or foreplay evolved into a relationship catastrophe. One party from the couple always emerged emotionally wounded and feeling like a third wheel. The awkward situation was heightened when that third wheel was the man. Never give a puppy a new bone and expect it to feign lack of interest. It really does not matter what sex the puppy is.

CHAPTER 18 ★ SEDUCTION PRODUCTION

This is not an area to pretend to be hip or cool about because any insecurity you are secretly harboring will be exposed. The only couple I had who successfully pulled off a fun night in the VIP room had chosen swinging as a lifestyle. Both parties were fully aware of what the other person was capable, and no one was unexpectedly thrown for an emotional loop.

## SCRIPT:

Ad lib!

# *Chapter 19*
# TOPLESS TERMS
*Learning a new lingo*

**Aug•mented Breasts** *n* : a surgical procedure that increases breast and wallet size, thus explaining the term "shake your money-makers"

**Cov•er Charge** *n* : monies paid for access to a club to see women remove their cover

**Gar•ter** *n* : much like a bank, it is a satin band worn around the dancer's thigh and holds money

**Lap Dance** *n* : not customarily performed on the main floor, this dance involves gyrating back and forth on a customer's lap

**Main Floor** *n* : normally consists of one large stage and several smaller stages where topless dancers perform in rotation to music

**Ped•es•tal** *n* : never to be waxed, this stool-like base is approximately two feet high and is used to support the dancer while performing a table dance

Reg•u•lar *n* : a man who has a predilection for topless bars

Sti•let•to *n* : customarily worn by trained professionals, these 4-7 inch heels look really good with a t-back

Sug•ar Dad•dy *n* : a man who has a predilection for a specific topless dancer

T-back *n* : Sisqó wrote a song about it: "the thong tha thong thong thong"

Ta•ble Dance *n* : a performance piece done by request (for a fee) directly in front of the patron on a pedestal

V.I.P. Card *n* : not to be confused with the Sam's club card, this card enables the customer to have certain discounts including entrance to the gentleman's club for them and their guests

V.I.P. Floor *n* : an exclusive area designated to provide patrons with added privacy and accessible only by payment of additional fees and/or the purchase of a bottle of champagne

V.I.P. Room *n* : more exclusive than a V.I.P. floor, this closed quarter provides more privacy than the law should allow.

*Chapter 20*
# CAMPAIGN SHOCK AND AWE
*What he doesn't want you to know*

The information found in this chapter should assist you in determining if your husband has graduated from the General Public. Most gentleman's clubs operate covertly regarding credit card transactions. Therefore, it is not standard operating procedure to find the words "topless bar" or "gentleman's club" printed on a receipt. For your convenience, I have provided an index of upscale clubs in the United States and a few in Canada, along with each company name as it lists during a credit card transaction. This tool may serve as a starting point; but if you discover your husband has evolved into a Regular or a Sugar Daddy, you may opt for professional help beyond the scope of this book.

## ARIZONA

| Name: | Appears on receipt as: | Location: |
| --- | --- | --- |
| Bourbon Street Circus | BSC | Phoenix, AZ |
| Le' Girls Cabaret & Café | Ziegfield Inc. | Phoenix, AZ |
| Tiffany's Cabaret | Sunset Entertainment | Phoenix, AZ |

## CALIFORNIA

| Name: | Appears on receipt as: | Location: |
| --- | --- | --- |
| Bare Elegance | Imperial Projects | Los Angeles, CA |
| Déjà Vu | Déjà Vu | San Diego, CA |

## CANADA

| Name: | Appears on receipt as: | Location: |
| --- | --- | --- |
| Cheetah's On The River | Lee Brothers Ltd. | Windsor, ON |
| Jason's | Aztec Tavern | Windsor, ON |
| Studio 4 | Ontario Ltd. | Windsor, ON |

## COLORADO

| Name: | Appears on receipt as: | Location: |
|---|---|---|
| Diamond Cabaret & Steakhouse | C.C.C.D., Inc. | Denver, CO |
| PT's Showclub | Denver Restaurant Corp. | Denver, CO |
| Shotgun Willie's | Bravada Inn Rest | Denver, CO |
| The Cheerleaders | The Morrison Company | Denver, CO |

## CONNECTICUT

| Name: | Appears on receipt as: | Location: |
|---|---|---|
| Elan's of Connecticut | Delmar Investments | Danbury, CT |

## FLORIDA

| Name: | Appears on receipt as: | Location: |
| --- | --- | --- |
| Club Harlem | HJ Enterprises | Winter Park, FL |
| Club Juana | Tinter Enterprises | Miami, FL |
| Dancers Royale | D&R | Orlando, FL |
| Rachel's North | Southeast Entertainment | Casselberry, FL |
| Rachel's South | Rachel's Steakhouse | Orlando, FL |
| Solid Gold | Golden Eateries | Sunny Isles, FL |

## GEORGIA

| Name: | Appears on receipt as: | Location: |
| --- | --- | --- |
| Cheetah Club | Alluvia Restaurant | Atlanta, GA |
| Gold Rush Showbar | Country Club, Inc. | Atlanta, GA |
| The Pink Pony | Trot, Inc. | Atlanta, GA |
| | | |

## ILLINOIS

| Name: | Appears on receipt as: | Location: |
| --- | --- | --- |
| The Doll House | Crazy Horse 2 | Chicago, IL |

## LOUISIANA

| Name: | Appears on receipt as: | Location: |
| --- | --- | --- |
| Gold Club | American Restaurant | New Orleans, LA |
| Larry Flynt's Hustler Club | Larry Flynt's Hustler Club | New Orleans, LA |
| Rick's Cabaret | RCIENT | New Orleans, LA |
| Temptations | Club Velocity | New Orleans, LA |

## MICHIGAN

| Name: | Appears on receipt as: | Location: |
| --- | --- | --- |
| BT's | Dearborn Avenue Bistro | Flint, MI |
| Landing Strip | NAPCO | Romulus, MI |
| Trumpps | D&W, Ltd. | Detroit, MI |
| Tycoons | Celebrity Reservations | Detroit, MI |

## NEVADA

| Name: | Appears on receipt as: | Location: |
| --- | --- | --- |
| Cheetah's Lounge | La Fuente | Las Vegas, NV |
| Club Paradise | C.P. Food & Beverage | Las Vegas, NV |
| Crazy Horse Too Topless Saloon | Power Company, Inc. | Las Vegas, NV |
| Palomino Club | Bermuda Sands | Las Vegas, NV |

## NEW YORK

| Name: | Appears on receipt as: | Location: |
|---|---|---|
| Flashdancers NYC | J.J. Cabaret | New York, NY |
| Paradise Club | Tarragon Enterprises. | New York, NY |
| Scores New York | Scores Restaurant | New York, NY |
| VIP | 8th Avenue Associates | New York, NY |
| Ten's | Gramercy | New York, NY |

## NORTH CAROLINA

| Name: | Appears on receipt as: | Location: |
|---|---|---|
| Leather & Lace | BL&L | Charlotte, NC |
| Leather & Lace North | L&L, Inc. | Charlotte, NC |
| The Diamond Club | DDD, Inc. | Charlotte, NC |
| | | |

## OHIO

| Name: | Appears on receipt as: | Location: |
|---|---|---|
| Christie's Cabaret | Entertainment U.S.A. | Cleveland, OH |
| Crazy Horse Men's Club | Milrick Corporation | Bedford Heights, OH |
| Penthouse Key Club | RES Enterprise | Cleveland, OH |
| The Gold Horse Cabaret | The Gold Restaurant | Cleveland, OH |

## PENNSLYVANIA

| Name: | Appears on receipt as: | Location: |
| --- | --- | --- |
| Delilah's Den of Philadelphia | D&D's Restaurant | Philadelphia, PA |

## RHODE ISLAND

| Name: | Appears on receipt as: | Location: |
| --- | --- | --- |
| The Satin Doll | Satin Doll | Providence, RI |

## TENNESSEE

| Name: | Appears on receipt as: | Location: |
| --- | --- | --- |
| Platinum Plus | Entertainment USA | Memphis, TN |

## TEXAS

| Name: | Appears on receipt as: | Location: |
| --- | --- | --- |
| Baby Dolls Saloon | D. Burch Management | Dallas, TX |
| Cabaret Royale | Millennium Restaurant | Dallas, TX |
| Caligula XXI | Here We Are Again | Dallas, TX |
| Gold Cup | DNW Houston, Inc. | Houston, TX |
| Hi-10 Cabaret | DHR, Inc. | Houston, TX |
| Michael's | Duncan Birch | Houston, TX |
| Million Dollar Saloon | Tempo Tamers, Inc. | Dallas, TX |

*(Continued)*

## TEXAS (Continued from previous page)

| Name: | Appears on receipt as: | Location: |
|---|---|---|
| Moments Cabaret | R&R Entertainment | Houston, TX |
| Naked Harem | Cosmopolitan Club | El Paso, TX |
| Rick's Restaurant & Bar | Trumps, Inc. | Houston, TX |
| Ritz Plaza | Steve's Steakhouse | Houston, TX |
| The Colorado Bar & Grill | Ice Embassy | Houston, TX |
| The Men's Club | TMC Restaurant | Houston, TX |
| The Men's Club | TMC Dallas Restaurant | Dallas, TX |

## WASHINGTON, DC

| Name: | Appears on receipt as: | Location: |
|---|---|---|
| Archibald's Gentleman's Club | HARCO | Washington, DC |
| Camelot Nite Club | RAH | Washington, DC |
| Joanna's 1819-Club | Snowco Enterprise | Washington, DC |

*Note: The author and/or publisher of this book do not assume liability for inaccurate listings due to misspellings, corporate restructuring or human error. Comprehensive information may be obtained through the corporate name database of each Secretary of State.*

# *Study Guide*

On the pages that follow, build on
the lessons of the previous chapters
as you develop plans to keep the
man you've got.

# CHAPTER 1: GUERRILLA WARFARE:

What convinced you that you and your husband were compatible and would be happy together?

How would you rate your level of enthusiasm regarding your mate on a scale of one to five, with five being highly excited and one being not excited whatsoever?

Name a favorable trait about your husband you can focus on that will help improve your level of enthusiasm about the relationship.

Write down three activities your husband and you enjoyed doing together that you haven't participated in since the "I do." Can you implement any of these activities into your routine again?

# CHAPTER 2: KNOCK OUT DROPS:

Are there any areas of your body that need special attention because of unpleasant odors?

Is your husband particularly fond of a fragrance you no longer wear? If so, consider buying that fragrance again.

Write down three ways you can improve the atmosphere within your home by catering to the sense of smell.

# CHAPTER 3: MP PATROL:

Designate and list the rooms in your home than can be used for family discussions.

What would you like your bedroom to represent?

Write down three things you can do to make your bedroom peaceful and clutter-free.

## CHAPTER 4: SIR, YES SIR:

Write down three barriers that are affecting your communication with your mate

When you and your mate have a disagreement, is it settled more often in a peaceable manner or in a shouting match? If you said shouting match, what can you do to help eliminate this negative pattern of behavior?

What is the least stressful time of the day and week for your husband? Choose this time to have important family discussions.

## CHAPTER 5: DAILY REVEILLE:

Describe the atmosphere inside your home in the morning.

Describe the atmosphere you want to help create inside your home in the morning.

Write down three tasks that you need to put into action that would help your home run more smoothly.

## CHAPTER 6: THE BATTLE LINES HAVE BEEN DRAWN:

Write down three qualities about yourself that make you proud. Celebrate, and give yourself a simple treat.

Write down an obstacle in the past that you were successful in overcoming. What was the defining moment that helped you triumph in that adverse situation?

Write down a quality you aspire to possess. What are your reasons for desiring this trait?

# CHAPTER 7: TRENCH WARFARE:

Write down three ways to play up your feminine assets at home.

In the past which of your outfits received the most compliments from your husband? Find an occasion to wear it again.

Which of your personality traits helps to strengthen the union between you and your spouse?

Which of your personality traits might contribute to weakening the union between you and your spouse?

# CHAPTER 8: RESTORE OR RETIRE:

Write down three changes in your personality that have negatively affected your relationship. How can you modify those changes?

Write down three areas where you feel you have improved over the years. Congratulate yourself and give yourself a treat.

Write down an activity of interest that you have been putting off for years.

What obstacles are preventing you from pursuing the activity above?

# CHAPTER 9: OUTRANKED:

What is the established hierarchy in your home at the present time?

Write down three qualities you admire in your spouse. Compliment, focus on, and nurture those qualities.

Write down a behavior of yours that may hinder your spouse's decision-making ability regarding crucial issues in your home.

# CHAPTER 10: KP DUTY:

Write down three ways to bring romance to the supper table.



Is there a chore that your husband performs that he would love you to carry out?



Is there a chore that you perform that you would love your husband to carry out?



Is it possible to perform a temporary switch of the chores above, or to devise an interesting reward upon completion of each chore?

# CHAPTER 11:
# DEFINING THE MISSION:

Write down the three most important tasks you perform for your family.

How do you grade your performance of each task?

What obstacles are preventing you from carrying out these tasks at peak performance?

# CHAPTER 12:
# REDEFINING THE MISSION:

Is there a major change brewing in your home?

What needs to take place to make the transition easier for your household?

Write down the names of family, friends and agencies that can offer additional support.

# CHAPTER 13:
# ALLIES AND ADVERSARIES:

Write down the names of at least two people whose advice you respect and solicit.

Is there anyone on your list who does not like your spouse? Remove anyone from your list whose advice does not benefit both you and your spouse.

Is there a couple in your community who could mentor you and your spouse? Plan an activity with them.

# CHAPTER 14: MORSE CODE:

Do you believe your promises to your spouse are consistent with your deeds?

Write down each of your verbal commitments to your spouse for 21 days. Cross them out as you perform them.

After 21 days has transpired, review your list of commitments. Does your original answer regarding deeds and commitments still stand?

# CHAPTER 15: EXPLORATION PARTY:

How often are you and your spouse making love?

On your present schedule, are the sexual needs of your husband being fulfilled to his satisfaction? If not, make adjustments.

Write down three ways you can improve love making in your marriage.

# CHAPTER 16: SWEET SURRENDER:

Write down three things you have argued about in the past that you are willing to let go. Let them go!

What behavior can you eliminate that would make the atmosphere inside your home more peaceful?

What behavior can you incorporate that would make the atmosphere inside your home more peaceful?

# MY MISSION STATEMENT AS WIFE AND LOVER
*(Write personal statement here)*

_____

_____

_____

_____

_____

_____

_____

_____

_____

_____

_____

_____

_____

_____

_____

_____

_____

_____

_____

_____

# 21-DAY COMMITMENT CONTRACT

I, *(insert name here)*_____, do hereby commit to being a more favorable wife by implementing the *Topless Tactics Plan* for a period of twenty-one consecutive days. My actions for the next twenty-one days will be consistent with the goals I have established for my marriage. I will not be moved by what I see or what I hear, nor will I be moved by the response I receive. I will be focused and ruthless in my execution to make my home a more peaceful place through compromise, sacrifice, compassion, good organizational skills, and most of all, love. I put all past offenses behind me because I choose to forgive. I will treat each new day with my spouse as a gift, and I will embrace that gift with the highest level of integrity that is in me. I will adapt. I will overcome.

Signature _____

Date _____

# IDEAS FOR GETTING ORGANIZED CALENDAR

| Morning | Noon | Night |
|---|---|---|
| Review and recite contract | Survey refrigerator and cabinets | Shop for groceries |
| Comb hair and change bedtime attire | Pick or purchase fresh flowers | Cook dinner (if you did not eat while out) |
| Cook large breakfast | Compose breakfast, lunch and dinner menu for the week | Iron for the week |
| Place handwritten love note on pillow complimenting husband about one thing you admire | Compose grocery list | Write down all appointments and promises in planner |
| Wake family | Compose weekly chore list for kids and post in a visible area | Check weekend homework |
| Eat together | Agree on a family outing | Put kids to bed at appointed time (all kids should be on a schedule regardless of age) |
| Straighten house as a family | Have fun! | Clean house and double-check alarm |

# IDEAS FOR SPECIAL DAY CALENDAR

| Morning | Noon | Night |
|---|---|---|
| Review and recite contract | Show up at office for planned lunch, indoor picnic and lap dance in husband's office (Leave map behind if you will be playing a game later) | Turn on the romantic music |
| Comb hair and change bedtime attire | Pick or purchase fresh flowers | Set kitchen table with wine and finger foods(cheese, fruit, shelled nuts, dip and assorted crackers) |
| Cook romantic breakfast (In cute costume if kids are away, if kids are home, improvise) | Double check prop list you created earlier in the week for your special day | Leave trail of flower petals from the front door to the main attraction area |
| Place handwritten love note on pillow complimenting husband's sexual prowess | Purchase any remaining items on list | Set the lighting |
| Wake husband | Purchase or perform manicure and pedicure (Clipped toenails are thoughtful if you are planning to have your toes sucked) | Locate the first aid kit (Stuff happens) |

*(Calendar continues next page)*

# IDEAS FOR SPECIAL DAY CALENDAR

*(Continued)*

| Morning | Noon | Night |
|---------|------|-------|
| Eat together | Remove all unwanted body hair (Don't be modest, you're married — Whack it!) | Set up remaining props and change into costume |
| Clean House | Take a hot bath with baby oil about an hour before your mate comes home (You want to be soft and fresh as possible) | Strike a pose |